Narrative Reading

1 What is the relationship between Daniel and Tim? How do you know

_____
_____

2 Why does Tim think the Birdman is a spy? **(1 mark)**

_____
_____
_____

3 In what ways does Daniel show courage? **(2 marks)**
(*Think about what he says and does.*)

_____
_____
_____
_____

4 Do you think Tim is right or wrong to threaten Daniel? Give your reasons. **(3 marks)**

_____
_____
_____
_____
_____

5 What do you think Gracie did next? Give your reasons. **(2 marks)**

'Why the Whales Came' and 'Wallie and Ollie': Bully, bully

Look at the description of Tim on page 4 and draw him as a cartoon character. Add a speech bubble. You can use words from the text or make up your own.

Now look at the first two frames of the cartoon on page 6 and describe the scene in words.

cruel   bully
menacing
sneering
mean
teasing
ugly

Author style and intent: Questions

1 Look at the first paragraph of 'Why the Whales Came' (page 4 in your **(3 marks)** *Revision Texts*). Write down **three** words or phrases that the author uses to describe Tim to make him appear threatening. (Look for phrases that describe how he looks and how he speaks, not what he says or does.)

- _____

- _____

- _____

2 Look at frame 6 of the comic strip 'Wally and Ollie' (page 6 in your *Revision* **(2 marks)** *Texts*). Mum asks Wally, 'Been crawling around with those creepies again?' Why does Wally reply, 'Hmmm you could say that!'

_____

_____

_____

3 Look at the endings to 'Why the Whales Came' and 'Wally and Ollie'. How do **(2 marks)** you think Wally feels? How do you think Daniel feels? (*For example, who do you think feels pleased? Who is hurt?*) Remember to refer to the text to support your answer.

_____

_____

_____

_____

4 What is the purpose of the pictures in the cartoon strip? **(2 marks)**

_____

_____

_____

Which story do you prefer? Write a paragraph below saying which you **(3 marks)** like best and why. Remember to refer to the text in your answer.

5

_____

_____

_____

_____

_____

_____

Narrative Reading

'The Tupilak': Questions

1 What happened to Quenna at the start of this **(1 mark)**
passage? Circle your answer.

She was pushed into the water.   She felt something heavy.

She was dragged out of the water.   She saw a body in the water.

2 How did Quenna feel when she got out of the water?   **(2 marks)**

_____

_____

3 Write down two things that Quenna saw when   **(2 marks)**
she opened her eyes.

- _____

- _____

4 Who does Quenna think the woman is?   **(1 mark)**

_____

5a 'She looked down. She was covered in furs... . A small fire burned brightly
close to where she lay.'
How long do you think Quenna was lying under   **(1 mark)**
the furs? Circle your answer.

seconds   a few minutes   about an hour   days

5b What makes you think this? Quote from the text.   **(2 marks)**

_____

_____

6 What made Quenna realise she was alive?   **(2 marks)**

_____

_____

_____

7 Look at the paragraph beginning 'The ice goddess had saved her life' to
'How long had she been in the ice palace?'
Why do you think the author uses questions in this passage? **(3 marks)**

_____

_____

_____

_____

_____

Notes

Revision
Texts
pp.7–8

'You Don't Look Very Poorly': Questions

Put a circle around your answers for questions 1-3.

1 This story is being told by Minna. How does she feel at the start of the extract? **(1 mark)**

suspicious   sorry   sick   silly

2 What does she expect from her mum? **(1 mark)**

coffee and chocolate biscuit   a bit of sympathy

a miniature steel band   an excuse

3 Why is Minna's mum suspicious? **(1 mark)**

Because Minna doesn't look poorly   Because Minna feels rotten

Because Minna is cross   Because Minna is sitting in the sofa

4 What made mum finally become sympathetic? **(2 marks)**

_____

_____

5 What was the matter with Minna? Tick **three** things. **(2 marks)**

☐ She had purple spots on her belly.   ☐ She was feeling shivery.

☐ She had trembling legs.   ☐ Her head was banging.

☐ Her hair was falling out.

6 What did Minna's mum do when she realised Minna was really sick? **(2 marks)**

_____

_____

7 Why do you think Minna was cross when her mum first brought in the tray? **(2 marks)**

_____

_____

8 How do you think Minna felt when she saw what was on the tray? **(2 marks)**
What makes you think this?

_____

_____

9 Different words are used to describe how characters speak. **Draw lines** **(2 marks)**
to show how the character is feeling or what they are trying to do.

soothed   angry

snapped   complaining

warned   trying to give comfort

grumbled   doesn't believe the other person

suspiciously   threatening

Narrative Reading

10 In what ways was Minna's mum a <u>good</u> nurse? **(2 marks)**

_____

_____

_____

11a Which character is telling the story? **(1 mark)**

_____

11b How does this influence the reader? **(2 marks)**

_____

_____

_____

'The Tupilak' and 'You Don't Look Very Poorly': Questions

1 Both texts are about someone who is sick. Which character would you **(3 marks)** prefer to be: Quenna or Minna? Explain your reasons fully using evidence from the text.

_____

_____

_____

_____

_____

2 Which story do you like best? Give your reasons using evidence from the **(3 marks)** texts. Think about the style of writing as well as the content.

_____

_____

_____

_____

CHALLENGE:
What do you think mum was doing while Minna was waiting upstairs?

_____

_____

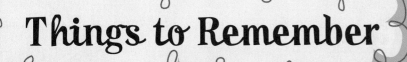

Things to Remember

READING STRATEGIES

When I come to a tricky word I can:

✔ Read on to the end of the sentence and think what would make sense.
✔ Chunk the word into syllables and sound it out.
✔ Go back to the beginning of the sentence.
✔ Read on in the text to see if there are further clues.
✔ Look for words within words or known parts of words.
✔
✔

When I am reading about characters I can think about:

✔ What they are saying.
✔ What they are doing.
✔ How they are speaking.
✔ How they look.
✔
✔

STRATEGIES FOR ANSWERING QUESTIONS

When I am reading questions I need to:

✔ Look for page or section references in the question.
✔ Underline key words or phrases in the question, such as 'what', 'who', 'why do you think'.
✔ Look at the marks awarded for answers. 1-mark answers may be information retrieval or deduction. 2-mark answers may require two pieces of information or require inference. 3-mark answers often require an opinion or explanation that goes beyond the text.
✔ Read questions carefully. Sometimes three pieces of information are required for one mark.
✔
✔

When I am answering questions I need to remember to:

✔ Work through the questions in order.
✔ Move on to the next question if I can't find the answer and go back to it later.
✔ Save time by answering with a word or phrase.
✔ Have a go at as many questions as I can.
✔
✔

Review and Targets

What I find easy

What I find hard

Strategies I can use to help

Targets
⊕
⊕
⊕
⊕

Teacher's comments

Narrative Writing

'The Spaceship': Planning sheet on character

What has happened?

_____

_____

Characters' names

Character 1: _____   Character 2: _____

Appearance

Character 1: _____   Character 2: _____

_____   _____

_____   _____

_____   _____

What are they doing? How do they move?

Character 1: _____   Character 2: _____

_____   _____

_____   _____

_____   _____

How are they feeling?

Think about how your character moves and speaks

Character 1: _____   Character 2: _____

_____   _____

_____   _____

What are they saying? How do they speak?

Character 1: _____   Character 2: _____

_____   _____

_____   _____

_____   _____

_____   _____

Words to Help:

stunned
amazed
terrified
frozen
crouching
hiding
quaking

Add your own:

Some speech verbs:

gasped
stuttered
yelled
whispered

Add your own:

13

Character Checklist

PHYSICAL APPEARANCE

✔	clothes – this gives clues about their personality and situation
✔	face – what is their expression like?
✔	size – this helps to compare/contrast them with other characters
✔	manner or demeanour – how do they hold themselves?
✔	
✔	

ACTIONS

✔	What is the character doing?
✔	How does the character move?
✔	
✔	

SPEECH

✔	What is the character saying?
✔	How do they say it?
✔	
✔	

Remember to describe:
- what your character looks like
- how they move
- how they speak

All these give clues to their <u>feelings</u> and <u>personality</u>.

FEELINGS

✔	Is the character happy/sad/excited/scared/troubled?
✔	
✔	

PERSONALITY

✔	Is the character kind/bullying/timid/brave?
✔	
✔	

'The spaceship': Characters

Write one or two paragraphs about the characters in the spaceship picture here. Use the plan you made on page 13.

Remember to include:
- Adjectives to describe the characters' appearance
- Verbs and adverbs to describe how they move
- Speech verbs to show how they speak

'Evacuees' and 'The haunted house': Description of setting

Can you make this description more interesting? It is a description of the setting illustrated in 'Evacuees' (page 13 of your *Revision Texts*.)

You could:
- Add more descriptive words.
- Change some words.
- Delete some words.

> We stood on the platform.
>
> The sky was grey.
>
> It was getting dark.
>
> The air was cold.
>
> We could see the countryside all around.
>
> It was different from the city we had left.
>
> I could just see my host family walking towards me.

The haunted house: Description of setting

Look at the picture on page 14 of your *Revision Texts*. Write brief notes below:

Where	When	What is it like?

Make the passage below more interesting. Add your own ideas.

> It was night-time. You could see bats against the full moon.
>
> The garden was overgrown.
>
> The house was set back from the road.
>
> It looked as if nobody had lived there for a long time.
>
> The windows were broken, the walls cracked. The chimney had fallen.
>
> At one window you could just make out the body of a person.

'The Cartoonist' and 'Truth or Dare': Openings and endings

Look at the openings and endings on pages 16 and 17 of your *Revision Texts*. Think about the strategies the writers have used to set the scene and draw the reader in. Think about how the endings keep the reader thinking. Write some notes below.

The Cartoonist

_____

_____

_____

_____

Truth or Dare

_____

_____

_____

_____

_____

Ways to create a good opening:

✔	I can talk directly to the reader.
✔	I can describe an unusual event.
✔	I can show characters talking to each other.
✔	
✔	
✔	
✔	

Ways to write a good ending:

✔	I can pose a question for the reader to think about.
✔	I can use speech to show a character's reaction to the events of the story.
✔	I can hint at what might happen next.
✔	
✔	
✔	
✔	

Anthony Jenkinson: Questions

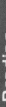

1 All three texts describe some of the difficulties that Anthony Jenkinson **(3 marks)**
encountered. Which do you think is most effective? Explain your answer.

_____

_____

_____

2 These sentences are taken from the three texts. **(1 mark)**
Match the sentence to the text it came from by drawing lines.

We saw distant bandits riding our way ... all well armed with bows, arrows and swords.	biography
In 1558 he voyaged for 4 months through Russian territory to the Caspian Sea.	magazine article
Completely out of contact with home, this brave merchant constantly took his life in his hands.	diary

3 The magazine article describes Anthony Jenkinson as 'A keen observer **(3 marks)**
of people'. Is this fact or opinion? Give a reason for your answer.

_____

_____

_____

4a What do you think the author's purpose was in writing 'Jenkinson's Journeys'? **(2 marks)**

_____

_____

4b How does the purpose differ from that of the other two articles? **(3 marks)**

_____

_____

_____

5 Which author's style and layout did you prefer reading? Explain why. **(3 marks)**
- 'Anthony Jenkinson – Tudor Explorer'   • 'Jenkinson's Journeys'
- 'From the Diary of Anthony Jenkinson'

_____

_____

_____

_____

Non-narrative Reading

6 How can you tell that 'Anthony Jenkinson – Tudor Explorer' and 'From the Diary of Anthony Jenkinson' were written by different people?   **(2 marks)**

_____

_____

_____

_____

7a Why does the author of 'Anthony Jenkinson – Tudor Explorer' describe Russia and central Asia as 'deeply mysterious'?   **(1 mark)**

_____

7b What effect does the use of 'fresh, sweet water' have on you and why?   **(2 marks)**

_____

_____

7c Under the sub-heading 'Fact-finding Missions' in 'Jenkinson's Journey's', the author adds the clause: '– even if their behaviour shocked or saddened him.' Why do you think he added this clause?   **(2 marks)**

_____

_____

8 Which title do you prefer: 'Anthony Jenkinson – Tudor Explorer' or 'Jenkinson's Journeys'? Give a reason for your answer.   **(3 marks)**

_____

_____

_____

'The Age of Discovery? <u>As If!</u>': Fact or Opinion?

- Fill in the columns with statements of fact or opinion from the text. One has been done for you as an example.
- Ask yourself three things: Did this actually happen? How does the author know this? Can I tell what the author thinks about this?
- Then use the Facts column to write a paragraph on the Age of Discovery.

Facts	Opinions
1492 – Christopher Columbus found an unknown continent	1492 – one of the saddest years

_____

_____

_____

_____

_____

_____

_____

_____

Text evaluation: Do you agree or disagree?

Choose *either* 'The Age of Discovery? As If!' *or* 'What Made the Dinosaurs Die?'
Write an evaluation of the author's viewpoint and then give your own.

- Tip: What is the <u>main point</u> the author makes? Is this a <u>fact</u> or an <u>opinion</u>?
- Tip: What facts support the main point?
- Tip: Is the author biased? What evidence is there of bias?
- Tip: Always refer to the text to support your evaluation.

Title: _____

The author claims that ...

_____

_____

He supports this by facts such as ...

_____

_____

_____

_____

_____

He shows his point of view by ...

_____

_____

_____

_____

_____

I think that ...

_____

_____

because ...

_____

_____

_____

_____

'The Day the Earth Was Hit for Six?': Questions

Answer the following questions about the text. Then say what type of questions they are, e.g. Literal, Deductive, Inferential or Evaluative, and how you answered them, e.g. skim-reading the text, using your own knowledge.

1 This text tells us that a meteorite wiped out the dinosaurs. True / False

Question type: _____

Method: _____

_____

2 Why are scientists getting excited about the discovery of the crater?

Answer: _____

_____

_____

Question type: _____

Method: _____

_____

3 Why does the author ask a question at the start of paragraph 4?

Answer: _____

_____

_____

Question type: _____

Method: _____

_____

4 Does the author express an opinion about how the dinosaurs died out?

Answer: _____

_____

_____

Question type: _____

Method: _____

_____

'Dinosaur Factfile': Questions

1 What is the origin of the word 'dinosaur'? **(1 mark)**

_____

2 Circle the correct answer. Dinosaurs lived on: **(1 mark)**

land   sea   air

3 What is the difference between _Compsognathus_ and _Apatosaurus_? **(1 mark)**

_____

_____

4 How do we find out about dinosaurs today? **(1 mark)**

_____

5 Why do you think the author uses the word 'interestingly' in line 7 on page 35? **(2 marks)**

_____

_____

_____

6 What is the main difference between the group of dinosaurs called **(1 mark)** 'Ornithischians' and the group called '_Saurischians_'?

_____

7 Before the 19th century, dinosaurs had not been identified as an **(2 marks)** extinct group of creatures. True or false? Explain your answer.

_____

_____

8 Which of these statements best describes the writer's purpose? **(1 mark)** Tick the best answer.

- ☐ to explain why dinosaurs disappeared.
- ☐ to describe how we can find out about dinosaurs.
- ☐ to describe the life-cycle of a dinosaur.
- ☐ to give us general information about dinosaurs.
- ☐ to list the kinds of dinosaurs and how they lived.

Give reasons for your answer. **(2 marks)**

_____

_____

_____

9 Why did Tyrannosaurus Rex prey on slower-moving dinosaurs? **(2 marks)**

_____
_____
_____

10 How can scientists work out what dinosaurs ate? **(2 marks)**

_____
_____
_____

11 'The age of the dinosaurs lasted for around 160 million years; then they all vanished.' Why do you think the author uses a semi-colon in this sentence instead of a connective such as 'and' or 'but'? **(3 marks)**

_____
_____
_____
_____

12 Why do scientists depend on fossils for information about dinosaurs? **(2 marks)**

_____
_____
_____

Things to Remember

PURPOSE (Which text-types have which purposes?)

✔
✔
✔
✔

STRUCTURE/LAYOUT (How does this help us read and understand the text?)

✔
✔
✔
✔

TEXT FEATURES (How do these features help us read and understand the text?)

✔
✔
✔
✔

LANGUAGE/VOCABULARY (What type of language is used and why?)

✔
✔
✔
✔

Targets

Teacher's comments

Non-narrative Writing

Revision Texts pp.36-37

CV Writing Frame

(Fill in the details as briefly as possible.)

PERSONAL DETAILS

Name:

Occupation:

Date of birth:

Distinguishing features:

Sex:

Marital status:

Education:

ACHIEVEMENTS (Write what you are good at.)

AMBITIONS (Write what else you want to achieve, and what you would like to do when you leave school.)

HOBBIES (Write what you do when you are not at school.)

Newspaper article

Headline – Keep it short and catchy, make readers want to read on, e.g. *Missing Holidaymakers Identified*.

Opening – Concise saying Who? What? Where? When?

Sub-headings – Four short sub-headings telling readers the content of the paragraphs, e.g. *Gloria Arkwright* etc.

Quotations – Include quotations from people who know the missing holiday-makers. Avoid using 'said' every time you quote someone, e.g. *sobbed a distraught fan*.

How much information? – Give key details from CVs – e.g. age, occupation. Use emotive language about people to increase interest.

Ending – Keep a sense of drama. Ask rhetorical questions, e.g. *Is time running out*

My Diary

Use this page to write about what happened to you in the lifeboat.

From the Diary of

Date

Describe what has happened and how you came to be in a lifeboat.
Think about the voice (first person) and verb tenses (past).

Describe who else is with you and what they are doing. Think about the tenses (present tense to describe appearances, and past tense to describe what they *did*).

Describe how you feel, and what you hope for. Think about tenses. You might use past, present *and* future tenses.

REMEMBER!
You are the writer *and* the audience.
Think about how to make your writing have a *personal* tone.

Non-narrative Writing

'Last Will and Testament'

Use the framework to write instructions to be followed about your possessions.

This is the last will and testament of

_____

I HEREBY (say what you are doing)

_____

_____

_____

I APPOINT (say who you want to carry out your will)

_____

_____

_____

_____

I ENTRUST TO (say what you want the above to do)

_____

_____

_____

_____

_____

I WISH THE FOLLOWING BEQUESTS TO (say who you want to have what)

_____

_____

_____

_____

_____

_____

_____

I HEREBY DECLARE (your final comment)

_____

_____

_____

_____

_____

Signed and dated

_____

Text type	CV	Last will and testament	Diary	Newspaper article
Layout and structure	autobiographical account headings, bullet points	numbered paragraphs		typographical devices
Language features	mixture of verb tenses		detailed, descriptive language	quotations